Featherstone

50 fantastic ideas for early writing prompts

ALISTAIR BRYCE-CLEGG

Featherstone
An imprint of Bloomsbury Publishing Plc

50 Bedford Square
London
WC1B 3DP
UK

1385 Broadway
New York
NY 10018
USA

www.bloomsbury.com

First published 2015

British Library Cataloguing-in-Publication Data
A catalogue record for this book is available from the British Library.

ISBN:
PB 978-1-4729-1325-8
ePDF 978-1-4729-1913-7

Library of Congress Cataloging-in-Publication Data
A catalogue record for this book is available from the Library of Congress.

10 9 8 7 6 5 4 3 2 1

Printed and bound in India by Replika Press Pvt. Ltd

This book is produced using paper that is made from wood grown in managed, sustainable forests. It is natural, renewable and recyclable. The logging and manufacturing processes conform to the environmental regulations of the country of origin.

Contents

Introduction

The minute children have grasped the fact that they can link sounds to these squiggly shapes called letters, things get really exciting for the emergent writer. No longer just a mark maker, they are now able to record symbols in a way that makes sense to them and that others can also decode and interpret.

This can be a very motivational stage for children's development, but it can on occasion cause children to stagnate and avoid writing. One of the many issues that they encounter is that there are lots of rules and exceptions when it comes to phonics that can take a little while (and a lot of effort) to master. The biggest inhibitors to children's success in writing are a lack of self-belief and motivation. Children who struggle with some of the early stages of the writing process very quickly come to regard themselves as 'bad' writers, and this is often not helped by the sorts of activities that we give children to promote effective writing. Children need to be highly motivated to write about things that they are interested in and enjoy.

In this book of **50 Fantastic Ideas for Early Writing Prompts** I have listed activities that I know have worked by firing children's interest and maintaining high levels of engagement. The activities are primarily aimed at children who are already on their writing journey, but they can easily be adapted either for your more emergent or else your more accomplished writers.

Food allergy alert

FOOD allergy!

When using food stuffs to enhance the children's play opportunities, always be mindful of potential food allergies. Look out for this symbol on the relevant pages.

Skin allergy alert

SKIN allergy!

Some detergents and soaps can cause skin reactions. Always be aware of potential skin allergies when letting the children mix anything with their hands, and always provide hand-washing facilities for the children to wash materials off after they have been in contact with skin. Watch out for this symbol on the relevant pages.

Safety issues

Social development can only take place when children are given opportunities to experiment and take reasonable risks in a safe environment. Encouraging independence and the use of natural resources inevitably raises some health and safety issues; these are identified where appropriate.

Children need help and good models for washing their hands when using natural materials or preparing food. They may need reminding not to put things in their mouths, and to be careful with real-life or found resources.

Hubble bubble

What you need:

- Spaghetti
- Plastic bag
- Food colouring
- Plastic or metal cauldron
- Various witch/wizard-related objects

What to do:

1. Cook the spaghetti as per the instructions.
2. When cooled, put the spaghetti into a plastic bag with a few drops of food colouring.
3. Agitate the spaghetti in the bag until completely coated in colour.
4. Pour the coloured spaghetti into the cauldron and mix in your wizardy objects!
5. Encourage the children to fish around in the cold spaghetti and pull out a writing prompt.

Taking it forward

- Use slime or gloop instead of the spaghetti – equally as effective, but just a bit messier.
- Vary the activity: the children could take out just one item or several, depending on the focus of your writing.

What's in it for the children?

This is a great activity to encourage the children's use of adjectives and rhyming words.

False teeth

What you need:

- A pair of false teeth

What to do:

There are hundreds of options at your disposal when it comes to false teeth! You could:

1. Link them to a familiar story.
2. 'Find them abandoned' in your setting.
3. Put them into an evidence bag.
4. Dig them up in your sand pit or garden.

Taking it forward

- As well as getting the children to write fictional stories about who the teeth belonged to and how they ended up in your setting, encourage them to write some non-fiction about human teeth and the teeth of other animals.

What's in it for the children?

You can use this activity to encourage both fiction and non-fiction writing, depending on where the children's interests take you.

Create a crime scene

What you need:

- Evidence of the crime
- Police tape
- Evidence bags

What to do:

1. Decide on the crime that is going to be committed.
2. Create a crime scene in your setting, leaving some obvious clues.
3. Tape off the area.
4. Let the children discover the crime and try to solve it.

Taking it forward

- Help the children to write a fictional account of what has taken place.
- Create 'Wanted' posters.
- Help them to write a crime report.
- Catalogue the evidence.

What's in it for the children?

Alongside descriptive writing, the children are also given the opportunity to practise their sequential and factual writing.

Letter from the fairies

What you need:

- Dolls' house furniture
- Writing paper and pens
- Small envelope
- Essence or scent
- Glitter (optional)
- Pressed flowers or seeds (optional)

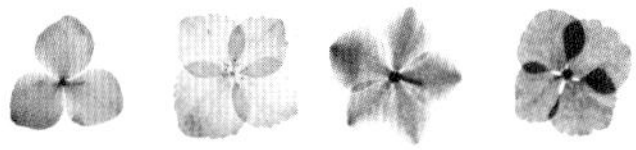

What's in it for the children?

This activity really supports the children in the development of their imaginations and their fantasy writing.

What to do:

1. Create a 'fairy scene' using dolls' house furniture.
2. Write your 'fairy' letter to the children.
3. Make the paper smell by adding scent.
4. Decorate it with fairy dust (glitter) and pressed flowers.
5. Leave the letter at the fairy scene for the children to discover.

SKIN allergy!

Taking it forward

Once the children are aware that they have fairies living in their setting, the possibilities for mark making are endless! They could:

- Write back to the fairies asking them questions.
- Write a fictitious account of what the fairies look like and how they live.
- Design and write instructions for a fairy-friendly 'fairy catcher'.
- Research and write about other famous fairy sightings.

Mythical book

What you need:

- Old hardback book
- Instant coffee (diluted) or brown shoe polish
- Ribbon or string
- Scissors
- Sealing wax and stamp (opional)

What to do:

1. Age the outside of the pages of your book with diluted coffee or shoe polish.
2. Snip and fray a length of ribbon or string using scissors to make it look worn.
3. Stain the ribbon with the coffee or shoe polish.
4. Tie the ribbon around the book and add any finishing touches such as a wax seal.
5. Leave the book in a chosen place in your setting for the children to find, explore and write about - see 'Taking it forward'.

Taking it forward

- Arrange to have the book 'delivered' to your setting.
- You could tell the children that it has been found in the depths of the library vaults.
- It could mysteriously 'appear' in your book box/library.
- The children could dig it up in their outdoor space.
- Generate ideas for their writing: what is in this book? Where did it come from? Should you open it?
- Again, the possible contents of this book are so open-ended that the children have numerous possibilities for writing.

What's in it for the children?

This is a really open-ended prompt, as the children's imaginations could take it anywhere: it could be a fantasy tale, a diary or a factual record…

Trapped!

What you need:

- Digital camera
- Printer and paper
- Scissors
- Laminator
- Card
- Sellotape
- Glue
- Plastic cup

What to do:

1. Take a full-length photograph of your children (get them to pose as if they are trapped and are pushing against invisible walls in front or to the side of them)!
2. Print the photograph, cut it out and laminate it.
3. Stick the photograph to a sheet of card by the feet so that it stands up (attaching with sellotape is easiest).
4. Put a small amount of glue around the rim of your plastic cup.
5. Stick the photograph to the inside of the cup so that the children look as though they have been trapped.

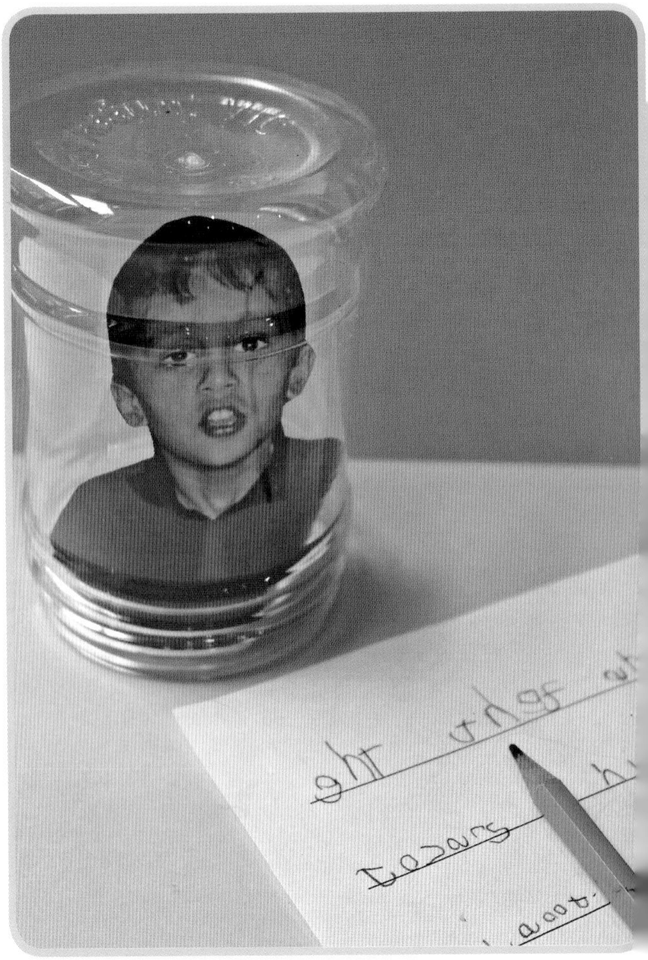

Taking it forward

Ask questions to generate ideas for their writing:

- Where have they been trapped?
- Who has trapped them?
- How did they get there?
- How are they going to get out?

What's in it for the children?

This prompt has endless possibilities and will really help the children to develop their imaginations and try to put themselves into an unfamiliar imaginary situation.

Six-word story

What you need:

- Whiteboard or paper
- Marker

What to do:

1. Tell the children that they are going to write a six-word story.
2. Ask them to count the six words out on their fingers as they say them.
3. Make sure there are lots of opportunities for the children to talk through their stories before they write them.
4. The story must have a beginning and an end and should make sense!

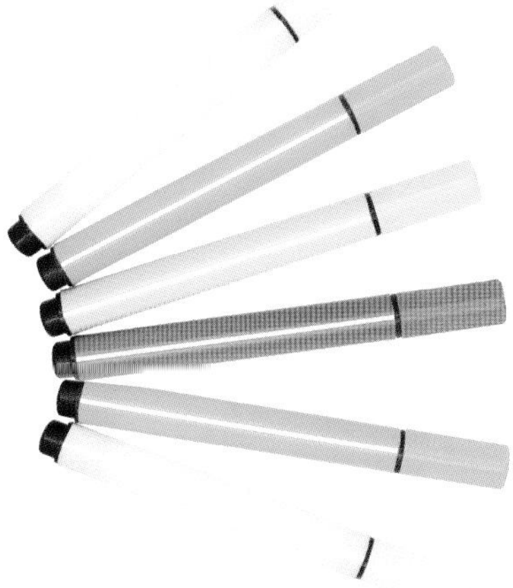

Taking it forward

- Try writing a six-word version of a familiar tale e.g. *Goldilocks*: 'Girl ate porridge, scared by bears!'
- Try writing a five or four-word story. The fewer words, the harder it is.
- Try creating a fictitious story with only six words.
- Join a number of six-word stories together to create a truly random tale!

What's in it for the children?

Writing a short story in this way encourages the children to really think about the structure and the words that they use.

Writing dice

What you need:

- Large dice
- Paper
- Glue
- Marker

Taking it forward

Have a go at:

- Changing the criteria on the dice.
- Using pictures instead of questions on the dice to inspire the children to create their story.
- Taking it in turns to throw the dice to create a shared piece of writing.

What's in it for the children?

This activity will familiarise children with many of the key aspects of fiction writing.

What to do:

1. Cut out six squares of paper to fit the sides of your dice, and use glue to stick them onto the dice.
2. On one of each of the sides of the dice, write:
   - Who am I?
   - Where am I?
   - Why am I here?
   - Who is with me?
   - What goes wrong?
   - How do I sort it out?
3. Encourage the children to roll the dice and use the questions as writing prompts.

Severed finger

What you need:

- Plastic ‘Halloween’ severed finger
- Bandage
- Red paint or food colouring (optional)
- Box or large matchbox

What to do:

1. Wrap the plastic finger in the bandage.
2. Add a bit of fake blood using food colouring or paint (optional).
3. Put the bandaged finger inside the box.
4. Let the children make their gruesome discovery!

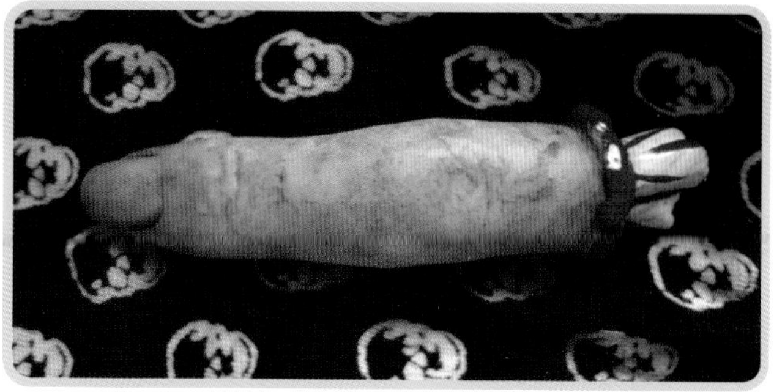

Taking it forward

Have a go at:

- Try using other ‘Halloween’ items such as witches’ fingers, or for a less gruesome activity use accessories such as a lost hat.
- Encourage the children to write about who the finger might have belonged to, how they lost it and how it has ended up in your setting.

What’s in it for the children?

Appealing to the more sinister side of children’s imaginations, this prompt is a great mechanism for creating and solving clues in a piece of writing!

Lolly stick prompt

What you need:

- Large lollipop sticks
- Permanent marker
- Sand
- Pot, tin, tub or bucket

What to do:

1. Write a prompt onto each lollipop stick using permanent marker. The prompt could be anything, from an interesting place to a popular fictional character or a favourite object.
2. Fill your containers with sand.
3. Put each stick into a tub of sand so that the text is hidden.
4. Children pull the sticks out of the sand and write about what they find.

Taking it forward

Have a go at:

- Replacing the words on the sticks with pictures.
- Having different coloured sticks – one colour for each aspect of writing.

What's in it for the children?

This prompt offers a new and fun opportunity for the children to take a random stimulus and apply their own writing techniques to it.

Ping-pong ball challenge

What you need:

- **30 ping-pong balls** (or as many as you have got children)
- **Permanent marker**
- **Jar or bowl**

What to do:

1. Write a prompt onto each ping-pong ball. This could be anything:
   - A person
   - An animal
   - A subject
   - A question
   - A situation
   - A place
2. The children pick a ball out of the jar at random and write about what is on their ping-pong ball.

'aking it forward

lave a go at:

- Changing the subject or criteria on the ping-pong balls.
- Having different coloured balls for different levels of challenge.
- Asking the children to choose a number of balls and incorporate them all into their writing.

/hat's in it for the children?

ıis quick-fire activity will encourage e children to use their knowledge of riting styles and mechanisms without arning or preparation.

Indoor campsite

What you need:

- Tent or fabric
- Wood
- Coloured paper (fire colours)
- Camping equipment

What to do:

1. Either put up a tent or create your own by draping fabric over an indoor structure.
2. Create a pretend campfire using wood, and coloured paper as flames.
3. 'Dress' your indoor campsite with camping equipment.
4. Encourage the children to engage in imaginary play.
5. Ask the children to write about their adventure.

Taking it forward

Have a go at prompting the children to:

- Write about where they are camping.
- Make up a funny or scary camping story.
- Write some jokes or ghost stories to tell around the campfire.
- Write their own camping song.
- Write some recipes for meals they could eat while camping.

What's in it for the children?

In this activity the children can either draw on the factual and familiar or can alternatively create the starting point for a fantasy adventure.

Picture prompts

What you need:

- Variety of different photographs or pictures
- Picture frames or menu holders
- Mark-making materials

What to do:

1. Put each picture/photograph into a frame.
2. Let the children select a picture that appeals to them.
3. Ask them to write about the picture that they have selected.

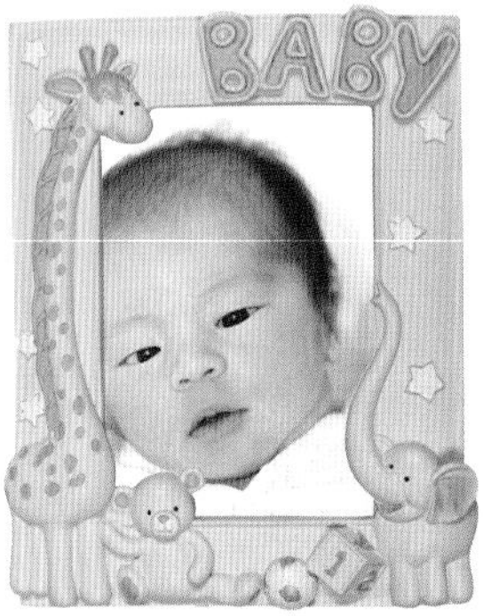

Taking it forward

Have a go at:

- Getting the children to work in groups to create a story.
- Including lots of talk time before the children start writing.
- Using pictures of past events that the children were involved in, to promote their engagement.

What's in it for the children?

This activity gives the children lots of visual stimuli to help inspire their writing. If they get stuck for words, they can always refer back to the picture for more ideas.

Message board

What you need:

- Pieces of card
- Laminator
- Low-level display space
- Sticky notes

What to do:

1. Make a card for each child by writing his or her name at the top.
2. Laminate the card for protection.
3. Stick the cards onto a low level display so that they are easily accessible by the children.
4. Children write each other notes, messages and stories on sticky notes and stick them to each other's cards.

Taking it forward

Have a go at:

- Adding a photograph of the child to their card.
- Adding a pocket to the bottom of each card for longer messages to be folded up and placed inside.
- Creating a message board for a fictitious or famous person for the children to message (you will have to message back!).

What's in it for the children?

This prompt is very much linked to real life and social interaction. It makes messaging purposeful, and will help to develop the children's writing skills.

Memory box

What you need:

- Small wooden or cardboard box
- Coloured or wrapping paper
- Pens and pencils

What to do:

1. Decorate your box using coloured paper or wrapping paper.
2. Either ask the children to write down a memory and put it in the box; or
3. Write down a number of memories from a variety of different situations - real and fictitious.
4. Ask the children to choose a memory from the memory box and write either a fictional or non-fictional version of it.

Taking it forward

- Collect the memories together and ask the children to create a diary for an imaginary person, using the memories as inspiration.
- Record the imagined memories of an animal, building or object.

What's in it for the children?

The children will be taking on the character of someone else and using their creative skills to express their thoughts and feelings.

If I had £50

What you need:

- **£50 note** (could be £20, £10 or £5!)
- **Photocopier**
- **A4 paper**

What to do:

1. Photocopy the £50 onto a sheet of A4 paper, keeping the note to scale.
2. Give the sheet the title: 'If I had £50…'
3. Create a writing and drawing space below the title.
4. Print off copies of the £50 activity sheets, enough for one per child.
5. Show the children the real money.
6. Have a talk session about what they would spend it on if it was theirs.
7. Encourage the children to record their thoughts on the £50 sheets.

Taking it forward

- Changing the amounts of money.
- Changing the title to 'If I had nothing'.

What's in it for the children?

This prompt encourages children to move between the realms of reality and fantasy in their writing.

Superhero power

What you need:

- A4 paper
- Mark-making resources
- Superhero picture/reading prompts

What to do:

1. Get the children to talk about what they know about superheroes.
2. Show the children some pictures of superheroes and superhero books.
3. Ask the children: if they were a superhero, what powers would they have?
4. Encourage the children to write a story in which they save the day with their super powers!

Taking it forward

Encourage the children to have a go at finishing the following sentences:

- If I was a superhero, the first thing I would do would be…
- If I was a superhero, I would look like…
- Introduce the terms 'villain' and 'nemesis' to the children. Ask them to complete the sentence: If I was a superhero, my nemesis would be called…

What's in it for the children?

This is a great way of developing imaginations, descriptive language and fantasy writing skills.

Best day ever!

What you need:

- A4 paper
- Writing materials

What to do:

1. Create writing frames on your piece of paper that say 'My best day ever', or help the children to create their own.
2. Leave space in the middle for writing and illustration.
3. Let the children write about their favourite day!

Taking it forward

Have a go at:

- Creating a class book of 'best days ever'.
- Encouraging the children to write imaginatively from the point of view of a fictional character, a historical figure or a celebrity. They could even write from the point of view of an animal, a building or a location.

What's in it for the children?

Whether the content is real or fictitious, this activity will help the children to order and sequence their work as well as biographically record their thoughts and feelings.

Magic cream

What you need:

- A cheap moisturiser
- Food colouring/powder paint/ liquid watercolour
- Essential oil or scent
- Jar or bottle
- 'Magic cream' label
- Writing resources

What to do:

1. Mix your moisturiser with your chosen colour.
2. Add your essence or scent and mix carefully.
3. Pour into a bottle or jar.
4. Label your jar 'Magic cream'.
5. Tell the children it is magic cream and ask them to write about what they think will happen when they apply it. (Remind the children not to apply it in real life.)

SKIN allergy!

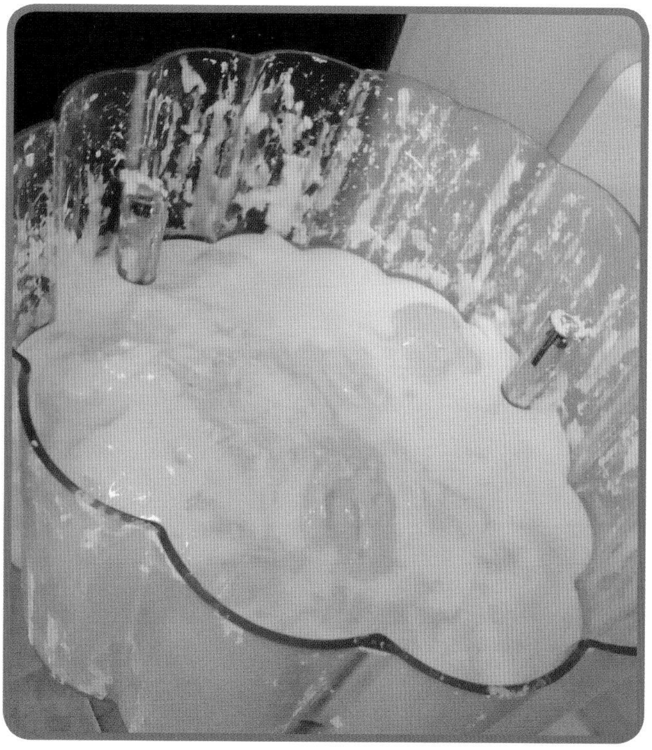

Taking it forward

Have a go at:

- Making your cream specific to a character, e.g. Wizard's cream or dragon's cream, by adding different colours and labels.
- Adding other ingredients such as seeds or beans that have a 'magic quality'.
- Adding some magic sparkle by using glitter or sequins.

What's in it for the children?

A fun way of developing children's imaginations, this prompt has endless possibilities – from real medical cures to fictitious and fantastic consequences!

Comic book templates

What you need:

- Tablet and comic book app or:
- A4 paper
- Permanent marker
- Ruler
- Comic books for reference
- Pictures and glue (optional) or felt tip pens

What to do:

1. Using either a comic book app or a marker pen and ruler, mark out the outline of a comic book page.
2. Repeat on several sheets of paper, creating slightly different sized templates.
3. Make sure that the children are familiar with a comic book layout – have lots of talk time before getting them started on the activity.
4. Using their imaginations, ask the children to create a comic book using one of the outlines.
5. Offer a selection of pictures for the children to stick onto their comic, or they could draw their own illustrations. Support them as they write the story for their comic strip

Taking it forward

- Use larger templates for less experienced writers.
- Make sure that the comic books you create appeal to all children.

What's in it for the children?

This is a familiar format for most children that will help them to understand how direct speech can be used to convey a story, and to apply this technique in their writing.

Inventor's box

What you need:

- Old box, chest or crate
- Variety of weird, wonderful and unusual objects
- Some tools
- Writing resources

What to do:

1. Put a whole variety of interesting objects in an old box, chest or crate.
2. Talk to the children about being an inventor.
3. Show them the inventor's box and let them explore it.
4. Discuss the uses of the various items in the box.
5. Tell the children they have to invent something using only the resources in the box.
6. Get the children to draw and label their invention and then create instructions for its use, using the tools as inspirational prompts for their writing.

Taking it forward

Have a go at:

- Asking the children to invent new names for familiar objects.
- Giving the invention a theme such as 'mouse catcher' or 'dragon fire extinguisher'.

What's in it for the children?

This prompt really gets children thinking and discussing, as they can't use their imaginations to create endless inventions in this activity: they have to be creative with the resources on offer.

Giant egg

What you need:

- Ostrich egg, plastic dinosaur egg or balloon
- Newspaper or kitchen roll
- PVA glue
- Paint
- Writing resources

Taking it forward

Have a go at:

- Encouraging the children to write a range of answers, getting children to think beyond 'dinosaur'.
- Leaving some other clues as to the sort of animal that might have laid it.
- Creating instructions for looking after a giant egg.

What's in it for the children?

Real or imaginary, fact or fiction? This scenario never fails to capture the imagination.

What to do:

1. If you are making your egg:
   - Blow up a balloon.
   - Cut the newspaper or kitchen roll into strips.
   - Dip the strips into PVA and cover your balloon (at least four layers).
   - Leave to dry.
   - Once dry, paint.
2. Hide your egg somewhere in your setting and let the children discover it.
3. Discuss with the children what might hatch out.

Alien spaceship crash

What you need:

- A variety of used car parts (see your local scrapyard or garage)
- Some circuit boards and wires – make sure they are child-safe
- Any other ambiguous bits of junk that you can find
- Spade
- Wooden stick or pole
- Green slime/gloop
- Letter, email, telephone call or newspaper

What to do:

1. Scatter all of the car parts, circuits and other junk (cleaned and without sharp edges) in your outdoor space.
2. Use the spade to part bury some of them so it looks as though they hit the ground with impact.
3. Use the wooden stick to create skid marks in the grass.
4. Pour large amounts of green slime liberally around the crash site.
5. Allow the children to discover all of the parts.
6. Tell the children there has been an email/letter/phone call/newspaper article explaining there have been some UFO sightings in the area.

Health & Safety

Remind the children to be careful when investigating the used car parts, and ask them not to run around the 'crash site'.

Taking it forward

Have a go at:

- Getting the children to create a 'Wanted' poster for an alien.
- Describing the planet where the aliens came from.
- Writing instructions on how to repair an alien spaceship.
- Writing a police report about the evidence collected.

What's in it for the children?

This prompt has a great air of mystery and engagement about it. It allows the children the opportunity to use their knowledge of fantasy writing, as well as lending itself to the more factual format of report writing.

Folding stories

What you need:

- A4 paper
- Pen or pencil
- Children in pairs or small groups

What to do:

This game has been around for a long time, but it is always a firm favourite for writing.

1. The children are going to take it in turns to write on the sheet of paper.
2. Each child will be given a different subject or criteria to write about, e.g. a person's name, a place, favourite food, random object or piece of clothing.
3. Once the child has written a word or phrase related to their criteria, they fold over a small section of the paper so the next child cannot see what was written before.
4. This continues until the paper is full.
5. Once the last child has had their turn, the paper is unravelled and the children have to make a story using the information that they have got on their sheet.

'aking it forward

lave a go at:

- Getting the children to talk through the information on the sheet first, so that they are clear about what they have to write.
- Linking all of the criteria to one subject rather than being random.

/hat's in it for the children?

ıis is a great game to play with ıildren as the outcome is so random. ıe more descriptive language they can ɜe, the funnier it is!

Invisible writing

What you need:

- Dandelions, lemon juice or bicarbonate of soda and water
- Thin paintbrush
- Paper
- Hairdryer (optional)

What to do:

1. If you are using a dandelion flower or lemon juice, you can mark make straight onto the paper.
2. If you are using bicarbonate of soda then you need to mix it with water to form a runny solution before you use it.
3. Once you have done your invisible writing, either let it dry in the sun, put it onto or next to a radiator, or blast it with a hairdryer on a hot setting.
4. As the heat dries, the invisible writing will turn brown and become visible!

Taking it forward

Have a go at:

- Sending secret messages.
- Inventing a secret code.
- Writing up a trial to see which invisible ink works best.

What's in it for the children?

This prompt encourages the children to really use their thinking skills, especially if they are writing in code!

Ransom note

What you need:

- Newspaper
- Glue
- A4 paper

What to do:

1. Cut out individual letters and words from newspapers.
2. Glue them onto a sheet of paper to form a ransom note.
3. Send the note to the children.

aking it forward

ave a go at:

- Getting the children to launch an investigation into who sent the ransom note.
- Asking the children to write back to the person/character that sent the note.
- Getting the children to create their own ransom note.

hat's in it for the children?

this activity the children will be able create a whole backstory about who nt the ransom note and why!

Message in a rock

What you need:

- 2 cups of flour
- 1 cup of salt
- 1 cup of water
- Mixing bowl
- 1 cup of soil or sand
- 1 cup of coffee granules (optional)
- Paper
- Writing materials
- Teabag
- Baking parchment
- Baking tray
- Oven

What to do:

1. To make the soil dough, mix the flour, salt and water together in a bowl.
2. Add the soil or sand.
3. Add the coffee granules (optional) – these will add colour and scent.
4. Stir into a dough, adding more water if necessary.

On the paper:

5. Write the beginning, middle or end of a sentence or message.
6. Rip the paper and scrumple it up to make it look old.
7. Dip a teabag in hot water and rub over the paper to make it look aged.
8. Leave to dry.
9. Once dry, take some of the soil dough and form it around the paper to create a stone or rock shape with the paper inside.
10. Place baking parchment on a baking tray and put the 'rocks' in the oven for around 40 minutes at 180 degrees, or until the outside is hard to the touch.
11. Once cooled, place the rocks outside and encourage the children to crack them open to reveal the secret message in each.
12. Encourage the children to finish the message or phrase in each stone.

Taking it forward

Have a go at:

- Encouraging the children to piece together various messages to solve a clue.
- Asking the children to create their own secret messages to put into 'rocks' like a time capsule.

What's in it for the children?

This writing prompt combines history with imaginative writing. The note they find could be from a real historical event or something completely made up!

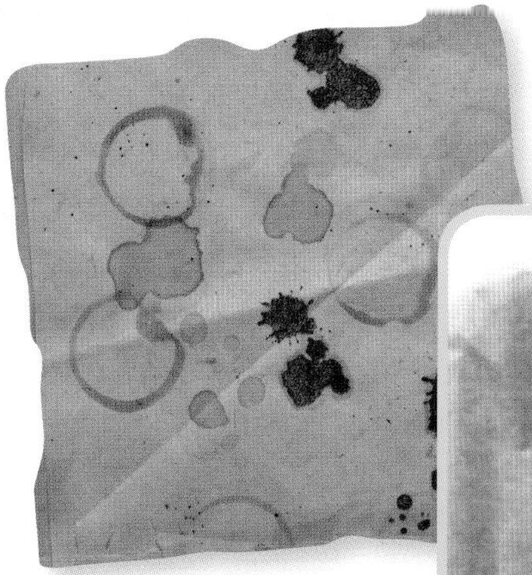

If you give an elephant an umbrella...

What you need:

Either:

- A collection of pictures of animals and a collection of pictures of objects

Or:

- An adult-generated writing frame with set combinations of animals and objects
- A collection of writing materials

What to do:

Either:

1. The children take it in turns to pick an animal and then an object.
2. The children then repeat the phrase: 'If you give a(n) (insert animal) a(n) (insert object)...'
3. The children then write about what could happen.

This can be done individually or in groups.

Or:

1. The adult pre-prepares combinations of animals and objects, and places them in a writing frame that the children can select from.
2. The children then use their imaginations and get writing!

Taking it forward

Have a go at:

- Expanding the idea to include other combinations.
- Getting the children to include more than one combination and use them to further develop their story.

What's in it for the children?

This prompt gets children playing with language alongside fact and fiction. The combinations are limitless, as well as the outcomes!

The best part of me

What you need:

- Paper
- Pens
- Scissors
- A4 sheets of card
- Camera
- Printer
- Glue

What to do:

1. Ask the children to write down what their favourite part of themselves is and why.
2. Mount each child's writing onto the bottom half of a sheet of card, under the heading 'The best part of my body is'.
3. Take a photograph of their favourite bit - alternatively, you may wish to encourage the children to draw a picture.
4. Stick the image above their writing.

Taking it forward

Have a go at:

- Getting the children to write about their favourite part of their friend.
- Getting the children to write about their favourite part of their family member.
- Asking the children to think about non-physical aspects e.g. sense of humour or kind personality.

What's in it for the children?

This prompt not only encourages writing as a means of expressing self-reflection, it also promotes positive self-image in children.

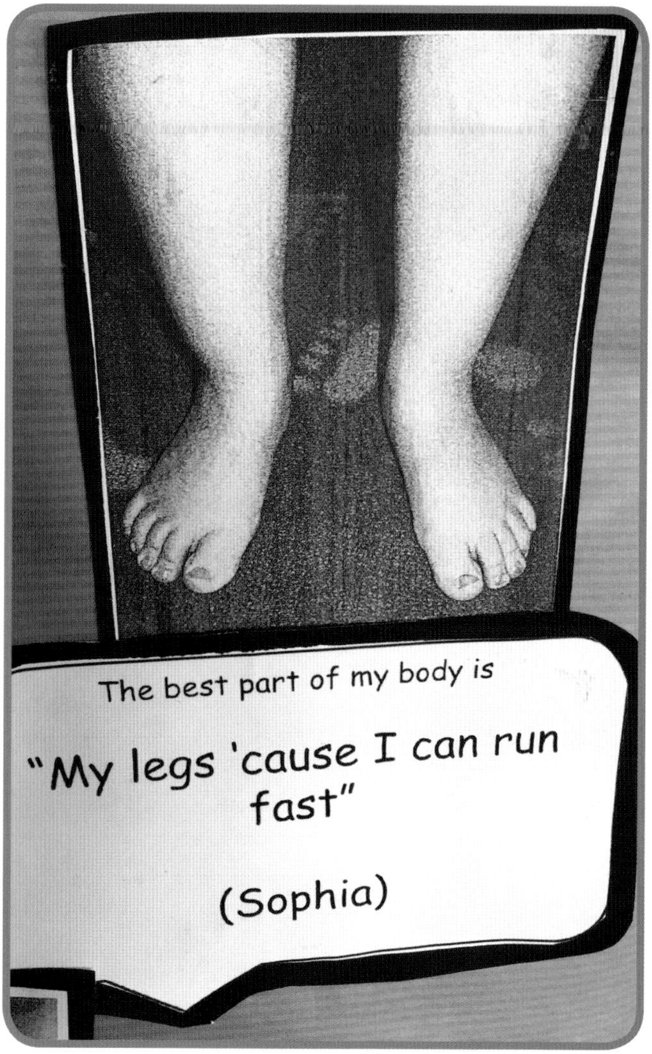

Dandelion wish

What you need:

- Dandelion in seed, or image of a dandelion flower
- Mark-making materials
- Lined paper

What to do:

1. Talk to the children about the tradition of making a wish as you blow the seeds from the head of a dandelion. They could say the traditional rhyme: 'Dandelion, dandelion puffs away. Make my wish come true some day.'
2. Ask the children: if they had one wish, what would it be?
3. Encourage the children to write about their wish.

Taking it forward

Have a go at:

- Taking a photograph of the children blowing the dandelion head to display alongside their writing.
- If dandelions are not in season, supply a pretend magic lamp and ask the children to make a wish by rubbing the lamp.

What's in it for the children?

This is a simple activity that will be very familiar to most children. You can encourage them to wish for something related to real life, or a complete fantasy.

Story towers

What you need:

- Construction bricks
- White stickers or address labels
- Writing resources

What to do:

1. Explain to the children that they are going to create a 'story tower'.
2. Each child will take it in turn to add another brick to the bottom of the tower.
3. Before they can place a brick in the tower, however, they must write the next sentence in your group story on a sticker and stick it onto their brick.
4. Read through the story together once the tower is complete.

aking it forward

lave a go at:

- Doing a simplified 'sentence' version for early writers.
- Colour-coding the bricks for different features of writing, e.g. if you pick a blue brick, you have to use an adjective.

/hat's in it for the children?

his activity helps to confirm for hildren the sequence of building a :ory – an essential skill for later writing.

Random word bottle

What you need:

- Plastic bottle
- Rice
- Freezer bag
- Food colouring (optional)
- Printer (optional)
- Laminator
- Writing resources

What to do:

1. If you would like coloured rice, put a plastic bottle's wort of rice into a freezer bag and add a few drops of food colouring.
2. Agitate the bag until the rice is coloured.
3. Empty the bag and spread the rice out to dry.
4. Print out or write a selection of words on pieces of paper that are small enough to fit into your bottle (make sure you print them double-sided). Use nouns, verbs, adjectives and adverbs.
5. Laminate your words.
6. Cut them out and put them into the bottle.
7. Add the rice, leaving a space at the top to allow the rice to move.
8. Get the children to shake the bottle and use the words that they can see as a prompt for their writing.

Taking it forward

Have a go at:

- Using longer phrases instead of single words.
- Creating 'beginning', 'middle' and 'ending' bottles for the children to use in turn.
- Creating different bottles for different features of writing.

What's in it for the children?

The skill here comes from the children's ability to be able to create something tangible from random words. It is a great activity to encourage the use of connectives.

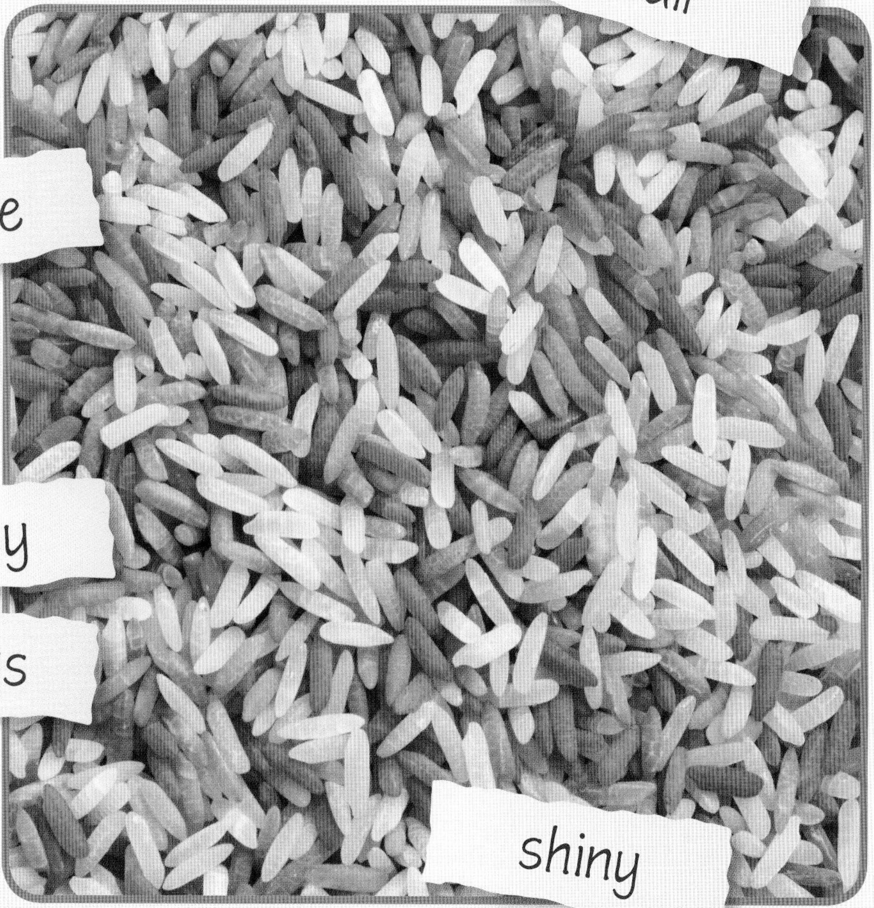

Code breaker

What you need:

- A pre-written code breaker (code breaker worksheets available on www.tes.co.uk)

Or:

- Photocopied sheet with a code that corresponds to letters of the alphabet
- Writing resources

What to do:

1. Talk to the children about the history of the use of codes and code breaking.
2. Show the children how to use the code that you have created.
3. Let the children write to each other in code and then decipher their messages.

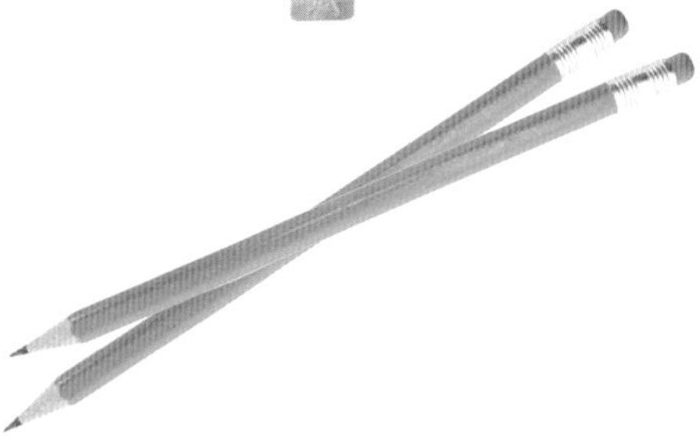

Taking it forward

- Let the children create their own code.
- Explore different kinds of code using letters, numbers and symbols.

What's in it for the children?

This activity usually initiates high levels of engagement, and supports the children's understanding of how words are structured.

Post box: this week posting to...

What you need:

- Post box, post bag or cardboard box with a slot
- Writing resources

What to do:

1. Tell the children that each week the post box will be for letters that are going to a particular person or place.
2. Link your people and destinations to children's interest.
3. Ask the children to compose a letter, poem or story to send in the post box.
4. Reply to the letters that are sent to maintain interest.

Taking it forward

- Encourage the children to try writing to real and fictitious people.
- Ask them to write to people from the past, present and future.
- Get them writing to their future selves, to remind them what it was like to be young.
- Try having a daily focus for the post box over a shorter period of time.

What's in it for the children?

This is a great prompt for looking at the skills of letter writing as well as aspects of factual writing, fiction writing and persuasion.

Typewriter: step back in time

What you need:

- Typewriter and typewriter ribbon
- Footage of typewriters in use (optional)
- Paper

What to do:

1. Talk to the children about how technology has changed. You may wish to show them a video clip of typewriters in use.
2. Show them the typewriter and talk about how it was used.
3. Allow them (the privilege) of typing out their writing on the typewriter.

Taking it forward

Have a go at:

- Borrowing a selection of different typewriters for the children to work on.

What's in it for the children?

Apart from a brief lesson in word processing history, it is an opportunity for the children to use another mechanism for the creation of their writing.

Popcorn writing

What you need:

- Yellow and white paper
- Writing resources
- Popcorn boxes/bags

Taking it forward

- Try having different popcorn boxes for different elements of writing.

What's in it for the children?

This prompt provides some structure that the children can then apply their best imaginative skills to.

What to do:

1. Cut up the yellow paper into small rectangles.
2. Write words or sentence starters on the paper.
3. Scrunch the paper up so that it looks like pieces of popcorn and place them in the popcorn boxes or bags.
4. Get the children to pick out pieces of 'popcorn' and use them as inspiration for their writing.

There was an old lady...

What you need:

- The song of 'the old lady who swallowed a fly'
- Picture cards (optional)
- Writing resources

What to do:

1. Play the song of 'the old lady who swallowed a fly'.
2. Tell the children that they will each be writing their own story that begins with 'There was an old lady who swallowed a...', and ask them to write down this starter sentence.
3. Get the children to pick a picture card.
4. Ask the children to complete their story by writing about what happened next, using the image on the card as a prompt.

aking it forward

ave a go at:

- Substituting the old lady for someone the children know, or themselves!
- Singing the songs out loud as a group.

hat's in it for the children?

is activity allows children to create a and new version of a song or story, odelled on a well-known tale. It can as inventive as they like!

Cloud spotting

What you need:

- A cloudy day
- Digital camera
- Printer (optional)
- Mark-making resources

What to do:

1. Go outdoors and get the children to lie on their backs with their eyes closed.
2. On your cue, ask them to open their eyes and look at the clouds (not into the sun!).
3. Each of them needs to try and identify a shape, person or object that they can see in the clouds.
4. Take photos of the cloud shapes, and when back indoors print the photos (optional).
5. The children use their cloud as the initial prompt for their writing.

Taking it forward

Have a go at:

- Composing a group story that involves all of the things that the children see in the clouds.

What's in it for the children?

The outcome of this activity all depends on how your children's imaginations work and what they see in the clouds. Don't expect any two interpretations to be the same!

Story bats and birds

What you need:

- Bat or bird template
- Card
- Scissors
- A4 paper in black (for a bat)
- A4 paper in various colours (for a bird)
- Writing resources

What to do:

1. Start by getting the children to draw around the template of a bat or bird onto card.
2. Cut out the template and cut a slit in the middle where the wings will go.
3. Ask the children to write short bat or bird stories on the paper. Encourage them to use bat or bird-related adjectives.
4. Concertina the paper.
5. Thread the concertinaed paper through the slit to make wings.

aking it forward

Have a go at:

- Using fluorescent markers for the bat stories, to make the wings glow in the dark.
- Hanging the bats and/or birds to create a screen in your setting.

/hat's in it for the children?

his activity involves art and craft reativity as well as writing. It's up) the children whether the writing is emed about bats or birds, or whether is more open-ended.

The key to a good story

What you need:

- **Luggage tags**
- **Keys** (real or cardboard cut-outs)
- **Jar**
- **Writing resources**

What to do:

1. Write a sentence on each luggage tag.
2. Tie each luggage tag to a key.
3. Place the keys in the jar and ask the children to take out one key each.
4. Encourage the children to write a story that includes the sentence on their key.

Taking it forward

Have a go at:

- Getting a group of children to work on the same sentence, to see how many different stories they can produce.
- Theming your keys around a particular genre or feature of writing.

What's in it for the children?

Here, the children start with the key as a prompt and a scaffold, as initially the story should begin by describing something that the key opens, or its owner. After that, imagination can take the writing in any direction!

Scavenger hunt stories

What you need:

- Small pieces of coloured card or paper
- Writing resources

What to do:

1. Write down one key element of a story on a small piece of coloured card or paper. Traditional stories work well, e.g. a wizard casting a powerful spell, a princess being rescued from a tower, or a fight between a hero and villain.
2. Repeat until you have a large selection of story elements.
3. Scatter the pieces of paper around your indoor or outdoor space.
4. Send the children to go and find a designated number of pieces of paper.
5. Ask the children to write a story using all of the elements that they have scavenged.

Taking it forward

- Colour-code your paper to different elements of writing and ask the children to collect one piece of paper in each colour.
- Organise both individual and group scavenges.

What's in it for the children?

This activity gets the children to really think about how they can connect random elements to make sense, using the mechanisms for writing that they have learned about.

Paint swatch stories

What you need:

- Selection of paint swatches
- Writing resources

What to do:

1. Ask the children to select a paint swatch (one card each, with each card containing a range of colour shades and their descriptive names).
2. Their task is to write a story or poem that includes all of the names of the colours on their swatch. Encourage them to use the names of the colours descriptively.

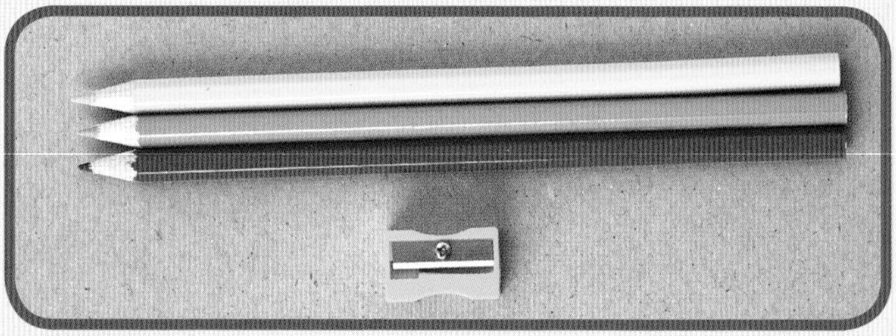

sunny

Taking it forward

Have a go at:

- Cutting up the paint swatches and mixing up the cards.
- Asking the children to write using a fineliner or felt tip that matches the colour of their paint swatch.

What's in it for the children?

Again, this prompt offers the children some initial structure to their writing and then relies on their imaginations to do the rest!

liberty

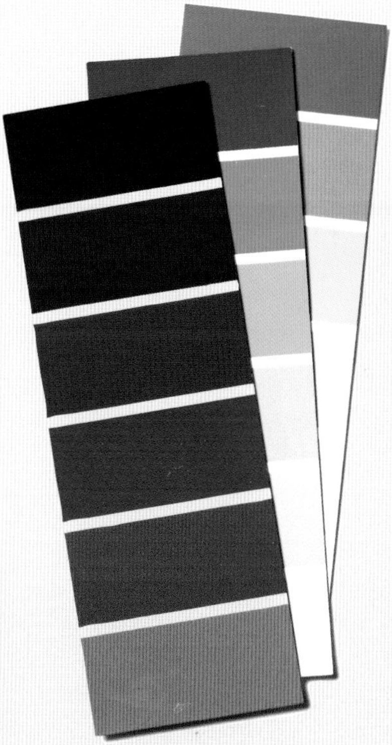

jungle

sky

coral

Story chains

What you need:

- Plain A4 paper
- Scissors
- A story/writing prompt (optional)
- Glue
- Writing resources

What to do:

1. Cut the A4 paper into strips (keep the strips wide for more emergent writers).
2. The children can work in groups or as a whole class.
3. Starting with the story prompt or children's own ideas, ask the first child to write a sentence or sentences on their piece of paper.
4. Once finished, the child loops his/her paper around with the writing facing outwards, and glues the ends together.
5. The next child carries on the story on his/her piece of paper.
6. When each child has finished their sentence/s, they loop their piece of paper through the one before it (the second being joined to the first loop, the third being joined to the second loop, and so on) to create a paper chain.
7. Once all of the children have finished, you will have a story chain. Always make sure that the writing is facing outwards and that the children leave enough room at the ends to glue together without overlapping any of the writing!

Taking it forward

Have a go at:

- Include 'adult loops' at points in the chain, which change the story.
- Have feature loops that say things like 'setting', 'character', 'adjective' etc. The adult can insert these at any point in the chain and the next child has to include that feature in their writing.

What's in it for the children?

You can't beat a bit of paper and glue when it comes to ways of getting a story going! This activity helps to reinforce the structure of writing and helps the children to understand how sentences link together.

Lost and found

What you need:

- Suitcase, shopping bag, handbag or carrier bag
- Items that tell a story or are linked to a character
- Writing resources

What to do:

1. Tell the children that you have had a delivery by mistake that was from the 'lost and found' at your nearest train station.
2. Show the children a suitcase or bag, or a selection of bags if you want to focus on more than one character.
3. Look at the contents of the bag together.
4. Talk about who the bag might have belonged to, and any character features that are indicated by the contents.
5. Ask the children to write about the owner of the case or bag.

'aking it forward

lave a go at:

- The children could write a biography, character description, newspaper article, lost luggage poster or fictional story.
- Return the item to its fictitious owner and receive a letter of thanks. Were the children right about the character?

'hat's in it for the children?

ıis is a great prompt for developing aracter; the children will learn how fferent objects might give us a clue to meone's personality and interests.

It's alive!

What you need:

- Live animal
- Writing resources

What to do:

1. Bring a live animal into your setting. This could be anything from a stick insect to a guinea pig.
2. Allow the children to have safe access to the animal.
3. The children can write about the animal itself or their own feelings about meeting it.

Health & Safety

Check whether the children have any allergies before bringing an animal into your setting.

Taking it forward

Have a go at:

- Bringing in unusual animals that the children might not have come across before.
- Using animals that are visible and interesting to observe, i.e. not hamsters who will burrow and sleep all day!
- Ask the children to write from the point of view of the animal on its first trip into school.

What's in it for the children?

Having a real animal sitting in front of the children is a very powerful prompt for their writing. If the children find that they are stuck they have a real live subject to refer to and to re-spark their writing genius!

Pick, stick, write and read

What you need:

- Photograph from each child
- A4 card
- Glue
- Writing resources

What to do:

1. Ask the children to pick a photograph from home that has some significance to them and bring it in.
2. Stick the photograph to the top of an A4 sheet of card (use a photocopy or scan of the photograph if necessary).
3. Ask the children to write about why their picture is significant.
4. Once complete, let the children share and read each other's writing.

aking it forward

ave a go at:

- Mixing the photographs up so that children are writing about someone else's photograph. Are there any similarities to the real story when they are finished?

'hat's in it for the children?

ecause this prompt is personal to ach of the children, it will give them ts to write about. Writing for an dience will help them to write in a ay that others will be able to interpret d understand.

Bucket list

What you need:

- A bucket
- Postcards or pieces of paper
- Writing resources

What to do:

1. Explain to the children that a bucket list is a list of things that you want to do before you 'kick the bucket'. Be sensitive to any children who might have lost a member of the family or friend recently when discussing death in this way.
2. Ask the children what they would most like to do in the world.
3. Get the children to write their idea on a postcard or piece of paper and put it into the bucket.
4. Children take it in turns to pull an idea out of the bucket.
5. Children write about the event, place or adventure.

Taking it forward

Have a go at:

- Changing the focus of the bucket: 'If I had one wish', 'If I were king/ queen for the day', 'If I were the headteacher'…

What's in it for the children?

This is a brilliant prompt for using the imagination. The children can choose whether to make their adventure real or to create a complete fantasy.

Scribble write

What you need:

- Newspaper
- Black marker pen (thick)
- Plain paper
- Writing resources

What to do:

1. Give each child a sheet of newspaper and a black marker.
2. Tell the children they are going to create a story, poem or sentence from their newspaper by scribbling out the words that they don't want.
3. Once finished, ask them to write out the words they have chosen on a piece of plain paper.
4. Display the two stories next to each other.

Taking it forward

- Try using the same technique to identify a particular aspect of writing e.g. connectives or adjectives, to then use in a longer piece of writing.

What's in it for the children?

This prompt will get the children to think about words, how they relate to each other and how they can connect them together. It is a great activity for learning about story sequence and connectives.

Once in a blue moon

What you need:

- Picture of the moon
- Light blue card or paper
- Photocopier
- Writing resources

What to do:

1. Photocopy the moon image onto the blue paper.
2. Explain to the children the meaning behind the phrase 'once a blue moon' (a second full moon in a month – usually there is one full moon per month. Neither are actually blue!).
3. Ask the children to write about something they do very rarely, and why they do it very rarely.
4. Ask the children to write a story about what might happen the next time there is a 'blue moon'.

aking it forward

lave a go at:

- Using other familiar or unusual phrases as a prompt for writing, e.g. 'never in a month of Sundays' or 'the camera never lies'.

/hat's in it for the children?

his is a great scaffold that usually has bit of 'magic' or 'mystery' about it. xpect werewolves and fairies as well s a bit of everything else!

Shower curtain short stories

What you need:

- Plain shower curtain
- Permanent marker
- Metre ruler
- Washable markers
- Strong waterproof tape
- Space!

What to do:

1. Using the permanent marker and a metre ruler, draw line on the shower curtain to look like the lined page of a notebook, including a margin.
2. Lay out your shower curtain so that it is completely flat. (You may want to tape the corners or around the edges).
3. Ask the children to take turns to come and start or carry on a story.
4. Ask each child to use a different coloured **washable** marker when they come and write.
5. Once the writing is finished you can wash the shower curtain and start again!

Taking it forward

Have a go at:

- Giving the writing a definite focus.
- Asking the children to illustrate their writing in the margin.

What's in it for the children?

This prompt helps children to understand the sequence of writing, but also how to make writing coherent by connecting it well and carrying on themes and ideas.